Industrial Relations and the Environment in the E.C.

EF/92/19/EN

European Foundation
for the Improvement of
Living and Working Conditions

Industrial Relations and the Environment in the E.C.

by
Eckart Hildebrandt

Loughlinstown House, Shankill, Co. Dublin, Ireland
Tel: 353 1 282 68 88 Fax: 353 1 282 64 56 Telex: 30726 EURF EI

Cataloguing data can be found at the end of this publication

Luxembourg: Office for Official Publications of the European Communities, 1992

ISBN 92-826-4687-4

© European Foundation for the Improvement of Living and Working Conditions, 1992.

For rights of translation or reproduction, applications should be made to the Director, European Foundation for the Improvement of Living and Working Conditions, Loughlinstown House, Shankill, Co. Dublin, Ireland.

Printed in Ireland

Preface

Industrial relations and the environment is a new topic on the agenda. Nevertheless it is a topic which is extremely suitable to be dealt with on a European level. The two sides of industry are confronted with an increasingly important problem for living and working conditions in Europe, which cannot be sufficiently solved by environmental policies of the national or supranational state. Environmental problems are not confined to a single company or enterprise, but have implications for regions, local communities and every single citizen. However, regulations, agreements and practice to improve environmental problems via the cooperation of different parties is not very strongly developed in the member states of the European Community.

On this background the European Foundation for the Improvement of Living and Working Conditions has started a cooperation with the Hans-Böckler Foundation in Düsseldorf in order to develop a work and research programme in Europe. The dissemination of the results and the cooperation of the researchers were also supported by the office of the Friedrich-Ebert-Foundation in Brussels.

The main objectives of this cooperation between the two German Foundations and the European Foundation are:

- to assess the importance of environmental problems for the social partners;

- to present different regulations and agreements on environmental problems on the sectorial and company level;

- to give an overview on the practice of cooperation between the social partners;

- to present examples of good practice.

The research programme was started with the creation of a research network in five countries. The members of the network are: Marc de Greef (Belgium); Denis Duclos (France); Eberhardt Schmidt (Germany); Andrea Oates (U.K.) and Alessandro Notargiovani (Italy). The project is coordinated by Eckart Hildebrandt from the International Science Centre in Berlin. He is also the author of the overview report based on the five country study which is presented here. Each country study can be sent out on request.

Based on the discussion with representatives of the Social partners on the European and national level, and national experts from 12 EC and non-EC countries and the European Commission a new work and research programme was developed for 1991/92. The existing country studies will be extended and more countries (10 altogether) will be added. Additionally seven case studies will be conducted.

Further publications from this project can be expected by Spring 1992.

Dublin and Düsseldorf,
October 1991

Hubert Krieger   Norbert Kluge
European Foundation   Hans Böckler Foundation

Table of Contents

	Page
Preface	1
Introduction	5
I. The status and development of industrial relations in European environmental policy	6
II. The research project	20
III. Industrial relations and the environment: the end of the latent phase	25
IV. Appropriate levels of action and forms of control	36
Bibliography	51

Introduction

Presented below are the first interim results of a research project, based on international cooperation, which examines the national foundations and international prospects of a European environmental policy resting on the independent activities of the social partners. The Single European Act has added to the EEC Treaty a subsection on environmental policy, with the aim of preserving and protecting the environment, and improving its quality. In this context, protection of the environment is regarded as a cross-sectional task impinging on the European Community's other policies. Accordingly, the European Foundation has included the theme of environmental protection in its four-year programme for 1989-1992, with attention focused on the company and its environment, among other aspects.

The principal aim of the present project is to complement central EC environmental policy by looking at the decentralized conditions and potential for the further development of environmental policy, and to suggest, in the light of this, incentives for supranational initiatives, measures and instruments. The qualitative improvement of environmental policy as it operates locally, and the establishment of a common EC environmental policy, are bound to be linked to the systems of industrial relations that have evolved.

The objectives of the project are threefold: first, to analyse the change in industrial relations accompanying the increased significance of industry-wide environmental problems; second, to analyse the globalization of national policies, or policy requirements, due to the opening-up of economic areas; third, to identify supranational approaches by the social partners to improving the protection of the environment.

The project initiated its survey with five national reports, which provide the basis for this interim report, and are published in a documentary volume. I express my thanks to Marc de Greef for the report on Belgium, to Denis Duclos for the report on France, to Eberhardt Schmidt for the report on the Federal Republic of Germany, to Andrea Oates for the report on the United Kingdom, and to Alessandro Notargiovanni for the report on Italy.

I. The status and development of industrial relations in European environmental policy

The prime motive for the project is the need to reinforce social innovative drive aimed at the protection of the environment. This implies, firstly, the promotion and elevation to a general level of environmental-protection initiatives and, secondly, the prevention of ecologically harmful dumping. Such innovative drive is defined by a number of different factors, including industrial relations in EC countries. Our assumptions are that there will, in the immediate future, be an increasing call for industrial relations to contribute to the strengthening of environmental policy (following the argument of a failure by central government to respond), and that the potential impact of these relations is, as yet, very far from having been realized.

I.I There are two models for analysing the **working mechanisms of international environmental policy:**

a. **The vertical model:** The initiative originates at international level, and measures are implemented from the top downwards. National and local measures have to wait until such time as the EC, for example, has adopted universally binding resolutions.

b. **The horizontal model:** Characterized by trail-blazers who do not wait for internationally harmonized measures to come into force. Innovations in environmental policy take place from the bottom upwards, originating in communes or regions, or at national level.

The experience gained so far shows that the vertical model is scarcely functioning - the higher the international level concerned, the greater is the mere verbalization of environmental policy. By contrast, there are good examples of national innovators who propagate their positive experiences internationally. Here, international organizations admittedly have great importance in the second step - the diffusion of pioneering efforts made at national level (cf Fig 1).

"The main thesis of the study is that forms of gradation, whether subject to a time limit or not, have proved themselves, in both theory and practice, to be the most successful approach to environmental policy. Such gradation embraces minimum standards and minimum goals, which may be improved on by particular countries; acceptance by some countries of the role of environmental innovators; or the laying-down of exceptional provisions for some countries, even though this may, on occasion, impair trade.

"This thesis flows from a political analysis of the European decision-making process as it has operated hitherto:

"Harmonization in Europe, aimed at affording a high level of protection to the environment, breaks down on national conflicts of interest. There is such diversity in individual European countries with regard to their state of economic development, their political systems and their social and political interests and alliances, that agreement on environmental policy is likely only in exceptional cases ...

"Adjustments usually demand a compromise between differing national interests - but seldom present a solution. The consequence is that the slow, clumsy and (so far as its content is concerned) inadequate decision-making process will continue to prevail in European environmental policy." (Hay-Böhm 1989, VI f)

In the Single European Act of June 1987, in which protection of the environment was for the first time incorporated into the EEC Treaty, the relationship between the horizontal and the vertical model is described. Article 100a provides for decisions to be taken by a "qualified majority". This means that measures can no longer be prevented by one Member State exercising its right of veto, and that national initiatives in the sense of more stringent provisions are permitted in certain circumstances (pioneering). With specific reference to environmental issues, Article 130 b calls for "unanimity", although it is up to the Council to define, on the proposal of the Commission of the European Communities and after hearing the views of the

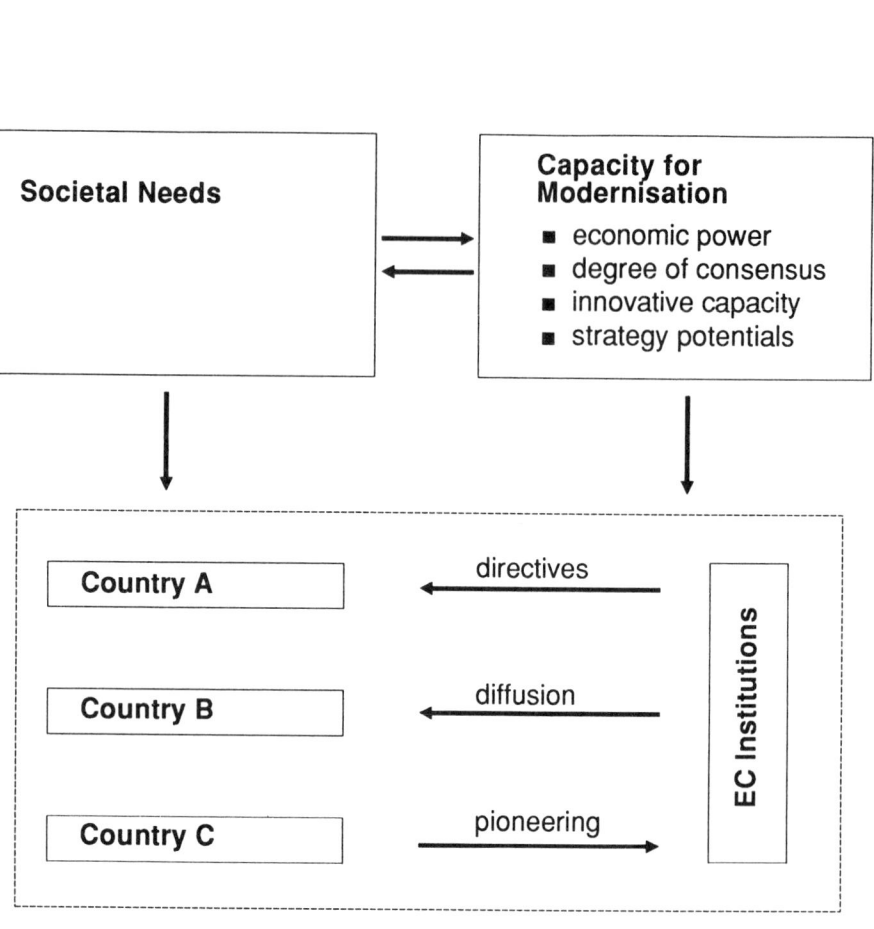

Bases of Environmental Policy in the EC — Fig. 1

European Parliament and the Economic and Social Committee, those matters on which decisions are to be taken by a qualified majority (Bongaerts 1989, 576 f.). This opens the way for the qualified-majority decision-making procedure to be applied to resolutions on environmental issues.

The productivity of both patterns - horizontal and vertical - is well illustrated by the example of the Federal Republic of Germany. On the one hand, it has sometimes required considerable pressure to convert EC directives into German law (as in the cases of drinking-water quality and testing for environmental compatibility). On the other hand, the Federal Government made early use of the provisions of Article 100a, sanctioning lone action, to play a pioneering role in banning lead from standard petrol grades. In the following, we concentrate on the horizontal pattern and exclude the EC-regulations from this presentation. This is also acceptable because th 5th action pgrogramme of EC environmental policy aims to more involvement of th two sides of industry, environmental organisations, consumers and local governments.

I.II It is therefore particularly important to gain a closer acquaintance with the **conditions determining the success of national environmental policy,** ie with the basic structural conditions for the development and diffusion of the continuing problem-solving process.

The identification of factors conducive to success has to take place retrospectively, just as the effectiveness of environmental processes which have run their course can be analysed only after the event. The basic conditions which have been found to exist in the EC countries are the outcome of historic growth and structural consolidation and cannot, in the short term, be manufactured or transplanted ("one best way").

Environmental policy is essentially a reactive policy. It presupposes an acute **problem-generated pressure** which can no longer be disregarded. Countries like Japan, the USA and the United Kingdom, which were early in setting up environmental institutions, drew attention to severe pollution of the environment in 1970, for example. This relationship is known as the **pollution-reaction thesis,** and it rests on two assumptions: firstly, that damage to the environment has recently increased, or undergone considerable structural change; and, secondly, that all environmental policy has come about as a reaction to increasing environmental pollution.

However, this explanation is insufficient, as many examples show (eg clean-air policy in Eastern Europe). It has to be complemented by a **capacity thesis**, according to which the development of environmental policy mirrors the state of socio-economic and politico-institutional capacities. Environmental policy is not merely a response to instances of pollution, but also reflects the resources available for their removal (Prittwitz 1990, 108). Jaenicke refers to this potential as **"capacity for modernization".**

Capacity for modernization is generally understood to mean the level of institutional and technical ability achieved by a country in resolving the problems connected with environmental protection (Jaenicke 1990, 221). Essentially, this encompasses four factors:

a. **Economic performance**

A high level of prosperity normally causes more environmental problems, but, against this, also creates better means of combating them. A low level of national development, or a crisis, has negative effects. A high level of economic development usually implies a large service sector, with the working population enjoying better education and more leisure, and this offers better potential for mobilization in the interests of the environment.

b. **Potential for consensus**

This involves the nature of the relationship between the government, capital and labour, ie whether the outcome of negotiations is generally broadly based (neo-corporatism), or whether uneasy conflict situations exist, or particular interests clearly predominate. According to past experience, "an active and cooperative interrelationship is more beneficial to the economy and the ecology than a laissez-faire philosophy" (Jaenicke 1990, 224). This regulatory system also covers industrial relations, to which I shall return.

c. **Innovative ability**

This concept essentially covers the material and institutional starting conditions for political and economic innovators. The institutional conditions include, for instance, the scope for the development of political attitudes, and equality of treatment before the law, ie the ability of ecological groups to make themselves felt within the political system, for instance. However, conditions which favour innovation tell us little about the institutionalization and implementation of ecological initiatives of this kind.

d. **Strategic capacity**

Environmental policy is a genuinely cross-sectional venture. In this context, strategic capacity refers to the ability of central government to orientate parts of the administration towards new goals, to defuse conflicts relating to objectives, and to integrate the policies of different parts of the system.

I.III Environmental policy is something relatively new, which has also introduced a change in political form. Traditionally, environmental policy has been seen as a matter for central government, which also guides the economic system by plans, legislation and measures affecting the infrastructure. However, experience in this area revealed such restricted potential that reference started to be made to a **"failure by central government"** (Jaenicke 1990). The reasons include the facts that

- central government is a weak actor in confrontation with the problems of the world market;

- political institutions are geared to a tradition of additive and reactive policy-making (contrary to the demand for preventive measures);

- an industrial-bureaucratic complex has evolved which, by agreement, seeks to solve problems by "bureaucratization" and "industrialization", leaving the solution of environmental problems untouched;

- the courts, which constitute the traditional forum for the clarification of issues, are increasingly overloaded.

For these reasons, there is a growing movement in favour of **negotiated settlements with the participation of the actors concerned,** ie alternative dispute resolutions. In these proceedings, far greater importance is assigned to the parties which are the cause of the issue, ie the business enterprises (subsidiarity).

Initial investigations indicate that the countries in which negotiating and participatory mechanisms have been developed are also more successful in environmental protection.

I.IV **Classical industrial relations** concentrate on the management of working relationships and the workplace. One of our central themes is whether, and how, an enterprise-related environmental policy can link up with the themes and rules of labour policy. Classical areas for such linkage are:

a. the coupling of environmental protection with the preservation or creation of jobs, and

b. the extension of health and safety at work to protection of the environment.

In principle, industrial relations can deal with work-related problems at different regulatory levels (cf Fig 2).

Traditionally, **three levels** are distinguished: the macro-level of national policy; the intermediate level of the branch or region, which is generally the domain of the negotiating parties; and the micro-level of the individual company or plant, at which there is direct interaction between company managements and representative bodies. EC environmental policy adds a fourth level, which normally affects the national level.

In the past, no account was taken of environmental policy at any level of industrial relations. However, depending on the country, the branch of industry and the size of plant involved, an increasing number of measures and initiatives have lately emerged, in which the actors engaged in industrial relations have been extending their areas of concern, and have been drawing in environmental issues and the actors concerned in these.

However, the basic facts remain that enterprises act without inclusion of their industrial relations, when taking strategic internal decisions or conducting their external relations, and that, internally, they limit the field of negotiation strictly to working conditions and work organization.

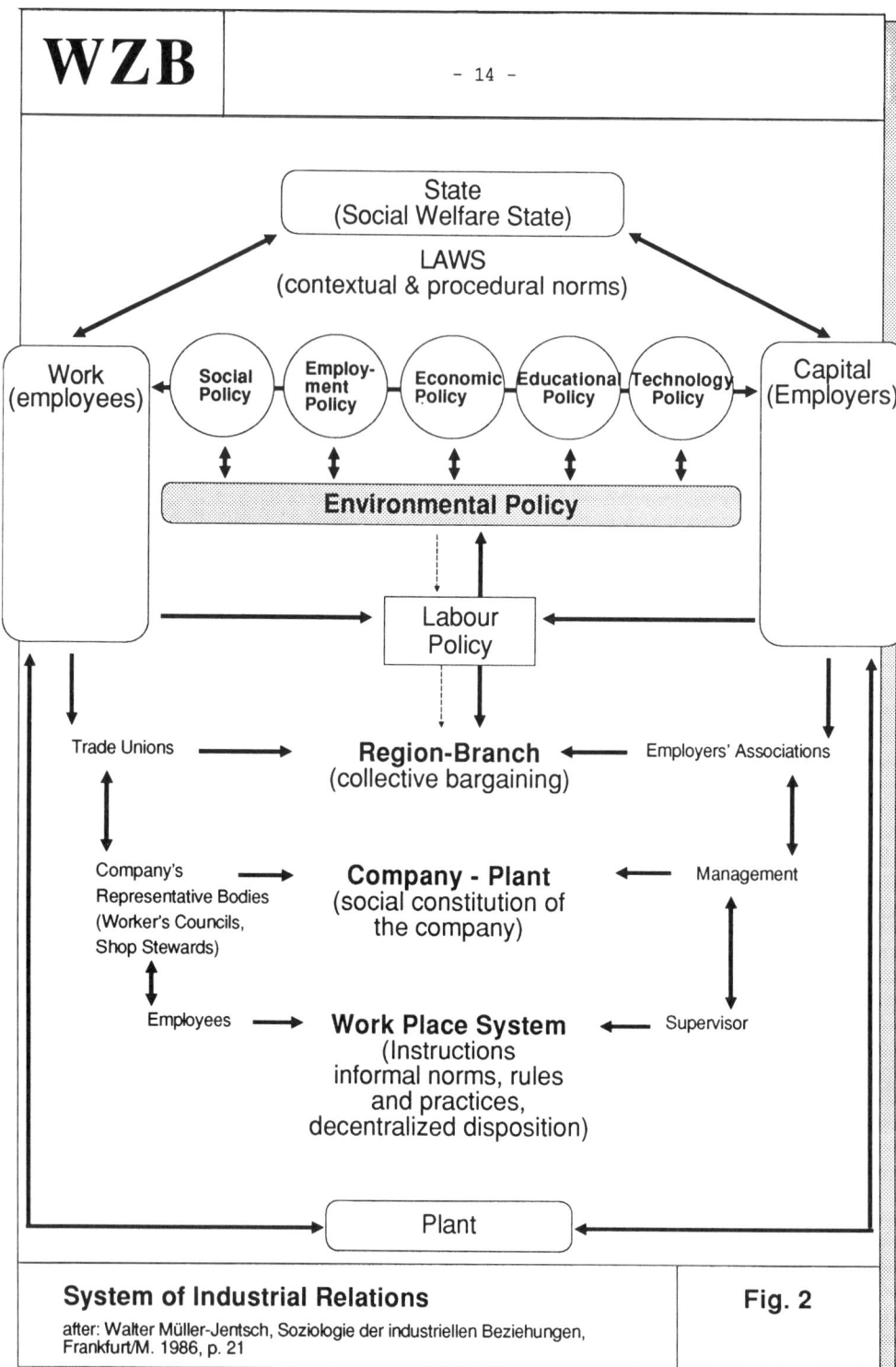

System of Industrial Relations
after: Walter Müller-Jentsch, Soziologie der industriellen Beziehungen, Frankfurt/M. 1986, p. 21

Fig. 2

The strict limitation of industrial relations contradicts two central findings of recent years. Firstly, **broadly conceived and cooperative industrial relations** have not merely raised working conditions to a high level, but have also had a positive effect on the international competitiveness of the economies concerned (eg Müller-Jentsch 1988). Secondly, environmental policy cannot be successfully conducted from the top on a centralized basis (eg Hoffman-Riem 1990).

We therefore find an increasing number of settlements of environmental conflicts in which **decentralized negotiating processes** operate between old and new actors, and between actors both internal and external to the plant. The research project concentrates on the question of whether, and how, the industrial-relations system is opening up to new actors, themes and forms of regulation, and is thereby changing, and adapting or isolating itself internationally.

There are, in principle, two ways in which organically evolved industrial relations can react to demands from outside for an ecological philosophy: they can bolt the doors against such demands, or they can open them. Bolting the doors could lead to the establishment of a new regulatory system additional to industrial relations, which would specialize in enterprise-related ecological problems. By contrast, opening the doors of IR to ecological problems would mean making linkages with existing themes and instruments, and progressively enlarging the area of concern.

For a systematic analytical appraisal, three dimensions of such an enlargement are important:

a. enlargement of the area of concern (cf Fig 3),
b. widening of the system of actors (cf Fig 4), and
c. extension of the forms of regulation (cf Fig 5).

Whether this expansion will take place, and how stable and far-reaching it will be, can finally be determined only by a large number of case studies and the analysis of new rules and institutions.

Interestingly, the processes of the transformation of industrial relations and the internationalization of environmental policy due to the consolidation of the European Community are combined in this context.

Thanks to five national studies within the EC and a large number of case studies, especially in the Federal Republic of Germany, we now have an initial body of material with which to examine the thesis of extended ecological engagement.

WZB — 17 —

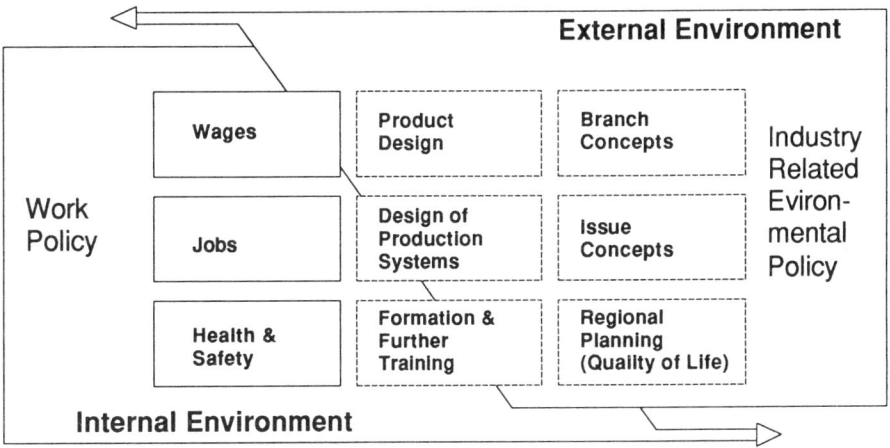

New Patterns of Industrial Relations I
Enlargement of work policy issues

Fig. 3

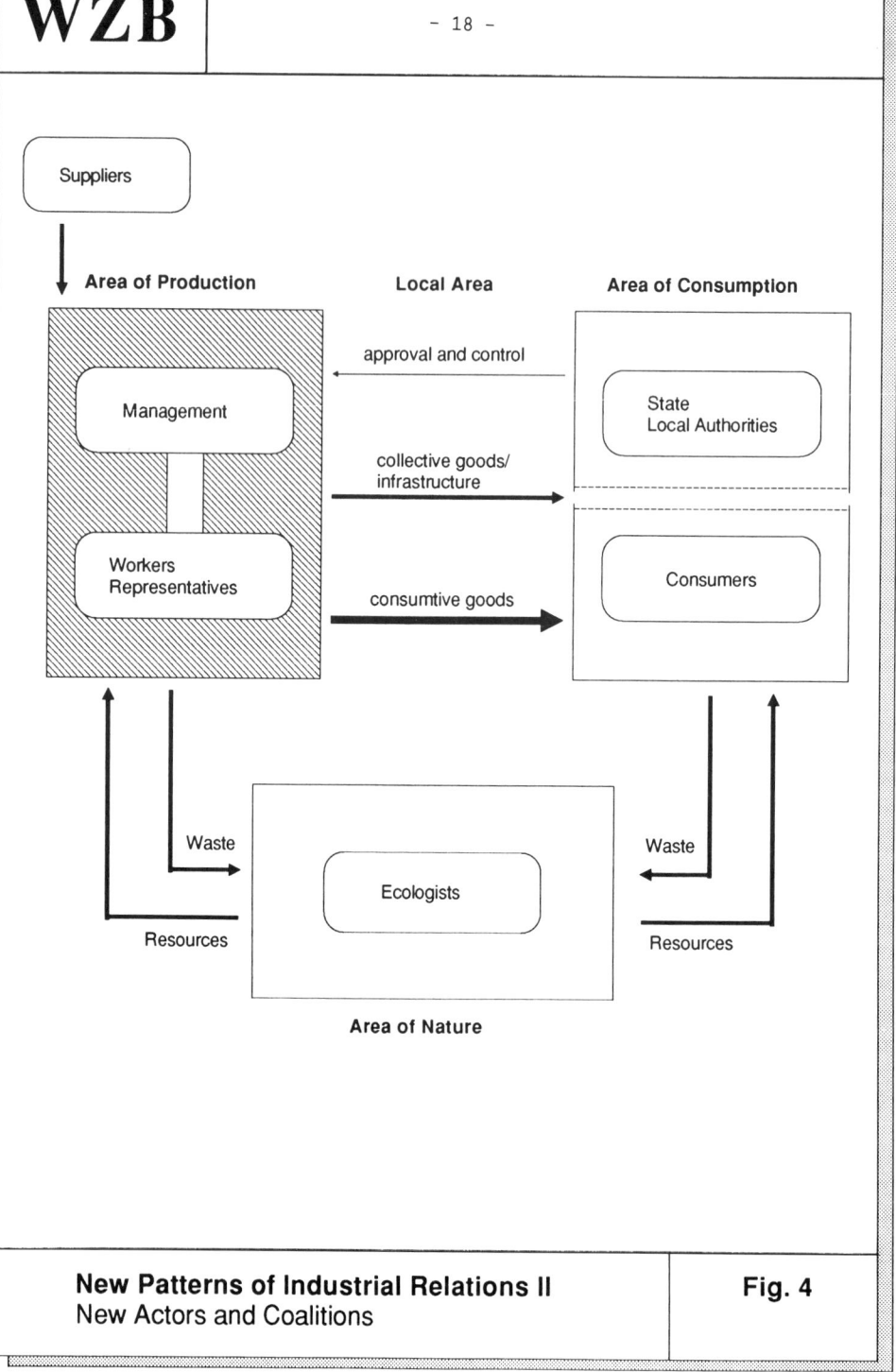

New Patterns of Industrial Relations II
New Actors and Coalitions

Fig. 4

Alternative Approaches to Resolving Distributional Disputes

Attributes	Conventional Approaches	Consensual Approaches
Outcomes	Win-lose; impaired relationships	All-gain; improved relationships
Participation	Mandatory	Voluntary
Style of Interaction	Indirect (trough lawyers or hired advocates)	Direct (parties deal face-to-face)
Procedures	Same ground rules and procedures apply in all cases	New ground rules and procedures designed for each case
Methods of reaching closure	Imposition of a final determination by a judge or an official	Voluntary acceptance of a final decision by the parties
Role of intermediaries	Unassisted; no role for intermediaries	Assisted or unassisted; various roles for intermediaries
Cost	Low to moderate in the short term; potentially very high in the long term	Moderate to high in the short term; low in the long term if successful
Representation	General-purpose elected or appointed officials	Ad hoc; specially selected for each negotiation

New Patterns of Industrial Relations III
New Forms of Regulation (Süsskind/Cruikshank 1987, 78)

Fig. 5

II. The research project

The research project "Industrial relations and the environment in the EC" was initiated in spring 1990 as a joint project of the European Foundation for the Improvement of Living and Working Conditions, Dublin, the Hans-Böckler-Stiftung, Düsseldorf, the Friedrich-Ebert-Stiftung, Brussels, and the Wissenschaftszentrum Berlin für Sozialforschung.

The **aims** of the project were as follows:

1. to examine the changes in the traditional systems of industrial relations in the EC countries due to the increasing significance of the environmental problem;

2. to identify the differences and common features of national structures and of the evolutionary trends in plant or plant-related environmental policy, and to assess their significance for the process of creating the common market;

3. to pinpoint the initial elements and central features of a supranational environmental policy, which builds on the industrial relations of individual countries, but at the same time meets present-day ecological needs and the challenges of the common market.

In an actor-related approach, the project tries to determine the contribution which can be made, independently and in cooperation, by an (ecologically enlarged) industrial-relations system to a future European environmental policy. This is in line with the self-awareness and environmental aims of the Community, which has laid down that its policy shall be based on principles including those of causation (the polluter pays) and subsidiarity.

In **the first phase of the project**, in 1990, five national reports (covering Belgium, the Federal Republic of Germany, France, Italy and the United Kingdom) were compiled on the basis of a uniform schedule of questions, and these were presented at the first workshop, held in Dublin in October 1990. They are published in this volume.

In **the second phase**, which was initiated by a second workshop in Brussels in March 1991, the analysis of the new patterns of industrial relations is being pursued in greater depth. This is supported, firstly, by expanded and additional national studies (planned to cover Denmark, Austria, the Netherlands, and possibly Spain and Greece), and secondly by specimen case studies in individual countries. The results of these studies, and of adjoining research, will be presented at a third meeting in Brussels in November 1991, and will be published later.

Depending on the results of the second phase, it is planned to devote a **third phase** to an analysis of the central issues affecting particular aspects of the environment, and of specific controls and instruments in the service of a new, ecological work policy.

The beginning of the project was marked by the national studies presented here with the object of providing a minimum body of information about the present state of the relationship between plant-related environmental policy and industrial relations. For this purpose, a network of scientists was built up, whose previous work placed them in a position to make at least an initial approach to interconnecting the following fields:

- national environmental policies,
- industrial relations,
- ecological corporate policy, and
- environmentalist groups.

And what was achieved was, indeed, only a start, since the subject involved not merely a new, and as yet scarcely demarcated, evolutionary trend, but also a new field of research. Those compiling the reports were therefore provided with a proposed method of arrangement, to ensure a uniform approach and coverage of the most important topics.

The **questions guiding the research** in this phase are as follows:

1. The national level to which environmental problems are explicitly formulated, and the accessibility of the industrial-relations system for establishing links with this new area of concern.

2. Central features of environmental controls broken down according to control levels (national, regional, local, branch, plant, workplace), and the nature of the measures involved (risk prevention, risk management and structural ecological strategy).

3. Central features of environmental controls broken down according to the actors and policy-making organs concerned (central government, companies, trade unions, communes), with particular attention to the involvement of environmentalist groups.

4. Evolutionary trends and predominant forms of control, with special attention to the significance of initiatives and agreements linked to industrial relations (unilateral, bilateral and multilateral measures); the relationship between regulations at higher level and individual initiatives (self-regulating potential of industrial relations); degree of legislative cover.

5. Prospects of linking environmental policy to business-management policy, and to health and safety measures; limitations of in-company environmental policy.

As already mentioned, the national reports that follow constitute an initial survey of the problem, and the formation of a body of data. They therefore exhibit a number of structural shortcomings which can be minimized only when the network has been cooperating over a longer period. For instance, the starting condition - that the problem area of "the environment and industrial relations" is something new - occasions considerable difficulties. Only to a limited extent can the research project rely on a theoretical approach

("ecologically extended work policy") and specimen case studies ("new patterns of regulating industrial relations"), which might be able to establish a shared basic understanding, and therefore a common method of addressing the subject. Instead, the central preoccupations of the past continue to predominate and govern the approach of the report-writers to the new research area. These older preoccupations are generally national industrial relations, with the emphasis on health and safety regulations. It is beyond question that important links exist between this issue and plant-related environmental policy, but there is also no doubt that it would be entirely one-sided and inadequate to confine companies' environmental protection policy to an extension of health and safety regulations. The universal distinction between environmental protection seen as internal and external to industrial plants focuses attention on this fundamental problem (cf Hildebrandt 1990).
The central concerns of the report-writers, and their methods of approach and interpretation, therefore hold greater sway than they would in an established field of inquiry. Another source of difficulty is that, because of the novelty of environmental initiatives in the industrial-relations system, it is, as yet, virtually impossible to assess which particular phenomena are important, what consequential effects they will have, and how long they will last. There is therefore a high degree of objective uncertainty affecting the evaluation and interpretation of new phenomena associated with the new requirements. Industrial plants are linked to, or the sites of, a multiplicity of developments, and it is, as yet, practically impossible to judge which of these will attain the status of effective strategies, instruments or institutions, and which are merely transitory.

The description of a policy area invariably suffers from inadequate differentiation between programme, measures, implementation and effectiveness. It is especially the case with environmental policy, in which the "realization shortfall" is symptomatic, and image-management and symbolic policy-making are of high importance, that the blurring of these differences can lead to serious misjudgements. According to the reports, the industrial-relations actors in the EC countries are at a stage in which a reorientation has occurred, which has moved them from a position of problem and responsibility evasion (externalization) to the position of accepting their contribution to problem creation, and active participation in finding solutions. In recent years, this has generally been reflected in the formulation of their own environmental action programmes. The future will bear witness to the extent to which these programmes can be implemented and the effectiveness of pilot projects and of the first cooperative organs.

A realistic survey must also take account of the structural and political obstacles which prevent employers' associations and trade unions from unbridled participation in environmental protection. The arguments of non-liability (laying the issues at the door of central government) and the incalculability of legal controls and of (international) competitive disadvantages are operative here, as are exorbitant environmental demands, the social defence of established rights, and conservatism in work policy. Difficult factors of this kind cannot be covered by the reports, but nonetheless affect the implementation of programmes and measures.

Lastly, there is a further difficulty. There are virtually no practical evaluative criteria with which the appropriateness of a measure to a given problem, and its environmental compatibility, can be gauged in the wider sense. There is therefore a danger that, concentrating on brief and sporadic reports of success (with regard to the duration, breadth and depth of the solution), one may be deceived about the progress actually made. This may be aggravated by a one-sided attitude which is widespread among IR researchers, that is to say, the overvaluation of formal regulations as opposed to informal rules and agreements, etc. It also appears to be one of the characteristics of successful environmental projects that they are substantially built upon the activities of the individual, using his own initiative, at a level below regulations, guidelines and technical solutions.

In view of the features of the national reports outlined above, their function for this first interim report is chiefly to provide a basis for the description of general patterns and evolutionary trends. The material is insufficiently detailed and exact to allow a factual comparison to be made between countries in the areas of particular issues, taking account of the relevant concepts and instruments. This is the objective pinpointed for the second phase of the project.

III. Industrial relations and the environment: the end of the latent phase

In characterizing social learning processes, it is helpful to identify individual phases of development. A three-phase model has proved basically suitable, in which a distinction is made between a latent phase, characterized by the emergence of the problem, without explicit formulation; a regulatory phase, in which the problem is taken up by various actors, and is dealt with either individually or collectively; and a consolidation phase, in which the method of dealing with the problem is generalized (higher level of environmental protection), and the newly constituted conflict-regulating mechanisms become firmly established, or disintegrate once more.

The national reports are, relatively speaking, at one in indicating that the subject of the environment has been a live issue for employers' associations and trade unions since about 1970, and that the level of awareness is generally high, although independent and more aggressive action had to await the end of the 1980s. Signs of this are the programmes and congresses of these organizations in which the environment is the central concern. By acting in this way, these associations do more than merely emphasize the importance of the subject, they recognize that they are directly concerned, and acknowledge their part in giving rise to the problem, and their obligation to participate in finding a solution. To this end, new areas of responsibility, environment officers, working parties and organizations are simultaneously brought into being.

This behaviour with regard to environmental issues contrasts sharply with that prevailing during the latent phase, which was characterized by the denial or passing-on of problems, and by sporadic measures taken by way of reaction.

It is clear that at this general level, at least, the division into periods, and the fundamental modes of behaviour of the social partners as regards the problem of the environment, reveal few differences between the countries being compared.

This uniformity is no doubt partly due to the range of countries so far selected. The sample comprises exclusively industrially highly developed countries with relatively strong economies and interest groups. The other pole of the Community's north-south gradient is not yet represented. Within our restricted range of analysis, it is apparent that the subject of the environment has been pinpointed and taken up on internationally parallel lines. With regard to the environment, the parties involved in industrial relations do not confront each other as opponents with a fundamentally different view of the problem and strategies for its solution, but are both exposed in a comparable way to pressure from outside, and they respond with entirely comparable modes of behaviour, although all act on their own behalf, and not within the industrial-relations system.

A universal finding expressed in the national reports is that the ecological bias to industrial relations has been accentuated by the interplay between government targets, the initiatives of environmentalist organizations, and the massive pressure exerted by the public media. A crucial role here has been played by environmental scandals with international repercussions (eg Chernobyl, Sandoz and Exxon Valdez), by problems affecting the global environment (eg the depletion of the world's ozone layer), and also by national scandals, which have heightened awareness of the problems and caused the efforts being made to deal with them to be stepped up. Even national environmental conflicts have common international dimensions, such as the problems posed by asbestos, and the emission of toxins into the atmosphere and in effluents. In West European environmental policy, there seem to be no basic country-specific features as regards either the emergence of problems, or the central issues involved.

For the actors engaged in industrial relations, the formulation of the problem in this way meant that most of the associated pressure came from outside. Their past behaviour was based on a kind of "productivity pact with externalized consequences". Industrialists and employees had reached implicit agreement that, or had become accustomed to a situation in which, the ecological consequences of their output, considered in the sense of the complete product cycle, should as far as possible be externalized, ie resources available free of charge should be used with prodigality, while resource costs should be passed on to the community, wherever possible on a cost-free basis, or they should be incurred there at the time of product use and disposal. It was not unfair to speak of a productivity pact between the industrialist and the trade unions at the expense of the natural world. The necessary consequence of the externalization policy is that the emergence of problems, and their explicit formulation, take place away from the plants, to which the problems - sooner or later - revert, as to their original cause. The aloofness and restraint of the social partners with regard to environmental problems is rooted, not so much in an absence of liability, as in an attempt to pursue the externalization policy (cf Fig 6).

Ecological Ignorance of Industrial Production

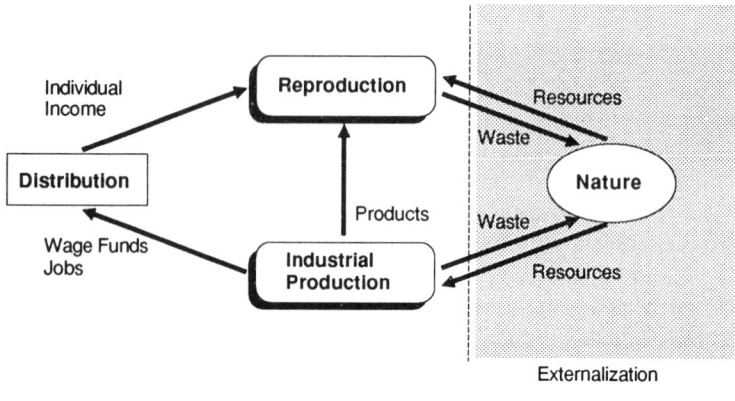

Ambivalence of Individual Roles

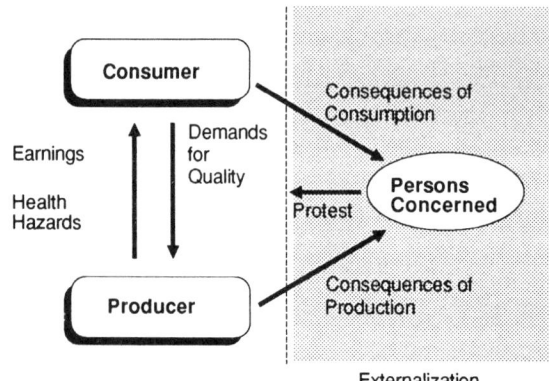

| Societal and Individual Modes of Externalization | Fig. 6 |

The basic forms of evasion adopted by industrialists and employees, together with their associations, in reaction to increasing external pressure can be listed as follows:

- **Dismissal of the issue,** ie the assertion that the claimed environmental danger does not exist, or does not exist in the alleged degree, or that the danger always existed, or that other hazards are far more serious.

- **Assignment of blame,** ie the allegation that other actors are the causative agents, and should be brought to book. Within the field of industrial relations, the assignment of blame to the industrialists by the trade unions plays a considerable role, as do the industrialists' recriminations against employees for negligent behaviour at work. More prominent, however, is the following tactic adopted by both parties:

- **Denial of liability,** ie protection of the environment is alleged to be a communal task, an aspect of the infrastructure and productivity for which the state is responsible. Such attribution of liability is additionally supported by the arguments for general and uniform starting conditions for enterprises, and by the costs incurred in setting, implementing and verifying standards.

- **Conservatism,** ie when associations respond to external pressure, they do so by reference to their existing policy, containing no independent environmental component. Environmental policy has been treated as a compelling question of time in terms of corporate programming, and in some cases measures have been taken under pressure. Generally, however, any independent liability for the environment has been explicitly denied, reference being made to the fact that the original objectives of the association indirectly constitute an environmental protection policy (technical progress, economic growth, health and safety regulations).

The last-named tactic of **reformulating** the subject of the environment to fit into the context of the (association's) own original policy framework is central, and ultimately signifies that an independent area of policy, "the environment", has not yet been created. The environmental policy of the associations is, in essence, **indirect and protectionist**. This also means that, while the associations react in similar manner to the ecological challenge, they do not do so collectively. The retreat to their own particular policy positions, and their defensive and rigid response, have offered no basis for a **cooperative policy**. As the reports show, the associations react selfishly, and only in answer to ecological problem situations presenting a concrete threat to themselves.

In the latent phase, **responsibility is characteristically attributed to the state.** It now transpires that, in the countries covered by the reports, there is firstly no uniform legislation relating to the environment, and secondly, the involvement of industrial relations in the state's environmental regulations has been highly marginal, if it existed at all. Environmental legislation, regulations and guidelines usually address particular aspects of the environment, and are specific in their effects. In the United Kingdom, the various laws have been brought together and unified since 1990, under the Environmental Protection Act, which provides a system of integrated controls for the different aspects of the environment. Although there have been widespread demands for unified legislationon the environment (for instance, by the Chemical Workers' Union in the Federal Republic of Germany), these have not yet borne fruit.

The role of the social partners in this legislation has been to participate in framing the various laws, and to ensure that they are complied with. Until now, industrial relations have played a marginal role here, as they are tailored to dealing with relationships within industry, which have hitherto not been taken to include environmental problems (cf, for instance, the German Betriebsverfassungsgesetz [Industrial Constitution Law]). Those acting on behalf of the state still cling to the separation of environmental policy and work policy, in other words to the principle that industrial relations should not be drawn into environmental policy. There has been some broadening of scope, with the enactment of stringent legal controls governing high-risk areas (eg in Italy), and a general increase in citizens' rights to information and participation (eg Law 349 in Italy, the right to the environment, and the laws controlling pollutants in the United Kingdom and the Federal Republic of Germany). Some trade unions are therefore looking for extended powers which stem less from increased rights to a say in the determination of economic policy than from a general reinforcement of citizens' rights.

All the reports emphasize that the provisions of **EC directives** have imparted a major thrust to environmental policy at national level and that, even in countries with comparably high standards, the adoption of these without attendant conflicts has not always been guaranteed. All in all, it is therefore fair to say that Community law generally exerts a progressive influence, and makes a substantial contribution to the standardization of otherwise very disparate rules and protection levels.

The question arises whether, in the next phase of open, active control, industrial relations will be allocated a more significant role in national environmental policy. This is suggested in some national reports; for instance, when the Belgian State Secretary for Environmental Affairs lays special stress on the role of companies and trade unions (report on Belgium, p 14), and when plans are made to extend the jurisdiction of health and safety authorities to environmental matters (eg Belgium, p 24).

The change in the organizations' environmental policy is therefore due less to compulsory enrolment in the state's policy-making process than to pressure from the other side. For business enterprises themselves, prime factors were clearly the requirements imposed by new legislation, which could not be circumvented in the longer term; the tangible pressure exerted by local supervisory authorities; also, conflicts concerning the quality of life close to factory sites, and more stringent criteria applied by customers and consumers; and, not least, the growing demands for a corporate culture inclusive of environmental issues (see, for instance, p 23 of the UK report) On the trade-union side, it is likely that the general change in priorities on the part of their members, and the practical local initiatives taken by them, have exerted the greatest pressure, and caused the subject of the environment to be addressed. At several points, explicit reference is made to the significance of critical consumers (UK report, p 14). The situation in which both employers and unions were questioned from outside about their public awareness, and about the "social and environmental compatibility" of their policies, led to the scene being dominated by reactions of legitimization vis-à-vis the outside world, and shrewd conflict-management, rather than by the solution of ecological problems.

The reports list an inventory of systematic points which explain why neither employers nor unions can commit themselves without qualification to an environmental protection policy. On the employers' side, the objections are generally familiar: legal uncertainties, costs, equality of competitive conditions, and areas of liability. On the trade-union side, the basic issue is that of compatibility, and, here too, massive barriers and opposing forces are at work: the varying impacts and differences of position within unions, conflicts between the protection of the environment and job preservation, lack of information about the environmental implications of industrial activities, and degrees of incompatibility between environmental protection internal and external to the company (UK report, p 11 ff).

All the reports make the point that the last decade, with its massive structural problems, the decoupling of economic growth and the labour market, the radical upheavals in employer/employee relations and staffing structures, and reversals of national regulative policies, has brought about a general weakening of the trade unions, which is not confined to the shrinkage in their membership. Growing economic problems not only cause attention to be focused on preservation of the status quo in the traditional areas of jobs and incomes, but generally diminish the ability of the trade unions to exert influence, even if they wished, explicitly, to speak with a powerful voice on environmental matters.

It is plausible that the emerging differences in national economic situations and the low level of regulatory intervention into company environmental policy will encourage a trend towards company-centred regulations (cf FRG, UK).

As all the reports remark, this means that **the individual enterprise or the individual plant** will become the central forum of industrial relations, the concerns of which will also cover the approach to environmental issues (cf Section IV for treatment in greater detail). The source of the influences which will come into play in this forum varies widely according to country (cf below).

The reports also provide some information about how the organizations approach the problem of the environment. As far as the employers' associations and individual enterprises are concerned, the centre of the stage seems to be occupied by organizational innovations (demarcation of liabilities, reinforcement of capacities), increased "green" marketing, and concentration on the technical side of environmental protection. The incorporation of environmental protection into factory and corporate planning, the institutionalization of environmental matters in the managerial departments of large corporations, and the concentration on "clean technologies" all point in the direction of autonomous management policy, and can be, especially in pioneering companies, very effective in single environmental issues. But simultaneously they exclude trade unions and employees from company environmental policy (cf, for example, the report on France, p 10). The name of the British action plan, "Environment means business", seems programmatic (UK report, p 23). In Belgium, too, it is still doubtful whether the joint statement by the employers' associations will also involve the trade unions (cf the report on Belgium, p 20). The initial approaches have been sufficiently developed in earlier joint campaigns and measures (eg Italy, p 20; UK, p 16; the German chemical industry), but the central negotiating role of industrial relations has, as yet, barely been addressed (see below).

Apart from general programmes, the trade unions concentrate their attention primarily on **particular problem-related campaigns** in areas which are also familiar in other countries:

- nuclear energy,
- carcinogenic substances,
- industrial diseases associated with asbestos,
- waste disposal,
- replacement of CFCs (chlorofluorocarbons), etc.

It is not sufficiently clear from the assembled materials whether these actions comprise independent and successful campaigns, or a contribution to wider national debates.

The other focal point lies in trade-union demands aimed at **enlarging the rights of industrial unions to information and participation** on the basis, and by extension, of existing national regulations governing health and safety at work. It strikes me as important that the extension of responsibilities and rights relates in the main to existing, representative organs based on an intricate division of labour, or, in other words, that social innovations in the sense of a participation-orientated organization of environmental protection are not really at issue.

It is apparent from the reports that the concentrations of company-related environmental management are to be found in the chemical industry and large corporations. The industry's overall impact on the level of environmental control is not, generally speaking, discernible. However, there are many indications that the chemical industry, as a comprehensive source of ecological risks which stands in the full glare of public criticism, is a focus for new regulations. This is a matter not only for campaigns involving individual companies, but also for sectoral agreements (cf the protocol of agreement and establishment of a national observatory in Italy, p 17; France, p 7; Belgium, p 25; and the central agreement in the Federal Republic of Germany). The metalworking industry is also of major importance, although this is chiefly due to its traditionally high level of politicization.

The concentration of corporate environmental initiatives in large companies is a general theme. This can generally be attributed to their superior financial standing, their greater functional specialization within the organization (with their own environmental consultants and departments), and the greater emphasis which they lay on public relations work and marketing. There are also indications that those representing interested parties within the company tend to feel a sense of relief when management assumes an active role, whereupon they react by abandoning this particular field, or henceforth exhibit a passive attitude. This, too, is a sign of the ambivalence of the roles being played in the protection of the environment.

IV. Appropriate levels of action and forms of control

All the reports agree that the company or plant constitutes the essential level at which corporate environmental policy is determined. This arises not, say, from any statutory provisions requiring that ecological questions are dealt with or negotiated in this forum, but, on the contrary, from the absence of any such provisions. The corporate level is crucial for three reasons. Firstly, corporate activity, the originator of risks and damage to the environment, takes place here, and a change in corporate policy reveals initial clues pointing to the ecological implications of company activity, so enabling ecological criteria to be incorporated into company policy, which is thereby rendered compatible with the environment. Secondly, the trade unions, or the employees' representatives, endeavour to use the institutionalized organs statutorily responsible in all countries for health and safety at plant level to gain access to environmental issues. Thirdly, trade-union campaigns concerned with pollutants, which are reported in almost every country, concentrate on implementation at plant level, ie on the avoidance, diminution or, at least, the halting at a fixed level of the use of pollutants in the plant. Within this framework, and independently within individual plants, a multitude of informal settlements and arrangements have been reached, which aim, in particular, at improving the in-company environment.

With regard to the extent to which there are, at plant level, independent statutory bodies concerned with environmental protection, the countries under consideration appear to exhibit considerable differences, which have not yet been sufficiently elucidated by the survey. The reports lay the main emphasis on the established health and safety organs, which rest on a statutory basis and, although the question of environmental protection doesnot explicitly form part of their remit, are automatically involved, at least in in-company environmental protection issues, thanks to the close link between safety at work and protection of the environment, especially when it comes to pollutants. Extending the activities of these organs (by environmental officers or committees) has hitherto depended on voluntary and cooperative practices within individual companies, and the extent of this process is obviously not fixed. The informal and pragmatic character of such an extension naturally imposes tight limits on its permanence and generalization.

The various countries also exhibit differences in the way in which, if it happens at all, the health and safety organs, whose central concern is to verify that the existing legislation and statutory provisions are complied with, liaise firstly with the chosen representatives of various interest groups within the company, and secondly with the company's trade-union representatives. In the United Kingdom we find an extreme case, in which the appointment of safety officers depends on trade-union acquiescence in the plant, and may, indeed, be undertaken by the unions (UK report, p 6). The opposite pole is represented by the German practice, where the various laws on the environment require the appointment of works environmental officers, who are responsible to company management and have hardly any links, in law, with the trade unions or those representing interest groups within the company.

While the reports universally consider the extension of company health and safety activity to the environment to be a hopeful development, the corporate position is likely to be decisively determined by management strategy. The increasing openness displayed by employers' associations and, more particularly, by individual companies in recent years points to an acceptance by company managements of responsibility for environmental policy, the setting-up of their own authoritative bodies, and the hesitant incorporation into company policy of aspects of environmental protection. The definition of environmental protection as a "management issue" (FRG) suggests that there is no general intention to involve the trade unions in working out a corporate environmental policy. The consultation of trade-union or internal company representatives occurs, if at all, informally at plant level. To date, there appears to have been no official ordinance requiring that such cooperation shall take place on matters concerning the protection of the environment. In the Federal Republic of Germany, an attempt to incorporate this new element into the Industrial Constitution Law actually foundered. Below contractual level, a large number of bilateral arrangements and agreements do, however, appear to exist in the various countries (for instance, in Italy), under which, at least officially, the subject of the environment is to be dealt with jointly. This is particularly liable to occur in those large corporations which attribute special value to projecting, internally and externally, the image of a cooperative corporate culture.

The importance of the **sectoral level** seems to vary very greatly. No doubt, it depends crucially on whether there are powerful associations (a system of industrial associations) at this level, and on whether the industrial-relations system attributes major significance to this intermediate level between national and corporate controls. It is clear from the reports that, because of the specific nature of the ecological problem, involvement in particular sectors of industry is gaining in importance. As sectors of industry are defined by products and manufacturing processes, they are naturally also associated with specific patterns of resource consumption, materials input and emissions. The multitude of anti-pollution campaigns conducted (sometimes in part) by the trade unions are therefore necessarily concerned with sectoral associations: the replacement of car paints, the reduced use of asbestos, the problems connected with nuclear energy, the replacement of solvents, the extension of waste-disposal systems, etc.

In most countries, the sectoral level derives some of its crucial importance from the fact that it is at this level that collective agreements covering industrial relations and working conditions are negotiated. The reports quote no instance, to date, of environmental issues having been incorporated in a collective agreement. From the FRG it is reported that the supplement to a collective agreement in the horticulture, agriculture and forestry sector obliges forestry workers to use environmentally benign gear oil in their power-saws. Apart from this, initial discussions on collective-agreement policy are under way in the metalworking industry, and a first draft has been prepared for a collective agreement in the food, drink and tobacco sector in the Federal Republic of Germany.

With regard to less stringent forms of regulation, however, there are already a number of bilateral agreements, which focus on the chemical industry. From Italy, for instance, a protocol of agreement and the establishment of a national observatory are reported (report on Italy, p 12), together with an agreement to conduct talks between the actors at plant level. In the Federal Republic of Germany, too, a central agreement has been reached in the chemical industry. This governs the information available to, and the capacities of, company works councils, and has led to many plant agreements along these lines.

Besides plant level, the sectoral level is also the one which attracts the concentrated criticism of the environmental-protection organizations. The opening-up of the trade unions to criticisms from green groups, and a growing recognition of their own incompetence in these matters, have led to initial contacts between unions and environmentalist organizations, with a view to devising an ecologically orientated sectoral and company policy. Examples of this are reported from the chemical sector and the metalworking industry in Italy and the Federal Republic of Germany, in particular.

It is at **national level** that decisions are taken regarding the level at which questions of corporate environmental policy are to be settled. Here, we find very wide disparities between the different countries. On the one hand, we have the French situation, where environmental concerns are a de facto state monopoly, although this has in recent years plainly generated a reaction in the sense that, side by side with powerful state intervention, independent forms of industrial relations have evolved (report on France, p 13). In Belgium, by contrast, the responsibility for environmental questions is explicitly assigned to the regional level, although it does seem that fairly comparable institutions and regulations have been established in the three regions. The situation is again different in the United Kingdom, where there is a tradition of non-regulation. Here, it is essentially the balance of forces and strategies at plant level which decides whether, and by what means, protection of the environment is to be incorporated into company policy.

Regardless of these great disparities between the national systems, it is apparent that the initiatives of the trade unions and environmentalist groups, at least, are directed towards more stringent national legislation in this area. The reports make it clear that the thrust is working in three directions: first, towards the target of a comprehensive, unified regulatory instrument enshrining a fundamental concept of the new approach to the environment (as in Italy); second, towards legislation laying down stricter conditions and controls for particularly hazardous areas and processes, with the participation of representatives of the interested parties; and third, towards the extension of existing legislation on co-determination rights in industrial plants, and towards a widening of the scope of industrial health and safety regulations to take in issues affecting the environment.

Relatively new and, with the exception of Belgium, subject to little regulation is the assignment of environmental questions to **regional, commune or local level**. The Belgian environment councils do, however, provide very good examples of the way in which industrial relations are opening up to other actors and new local regulations. It is reported that, in the Walloon region, the environment council consists not only of environmental delegates and experts from the universities, but also of representatives of the towns, communes, consumer organizations and the social partners (report on Belgium, pp 6-7). The report on Italy mentions consultation procedures at local level concerned with regional planning, water supply, and transport and waste-disposal systems, together with debates on locations, and such issues as air and water quality and recreation areas in towns. At the negotiation of the Lombardy Agreement, on the improvement of air and water quality in Val Chiavenna, the parties represented included companies, industrial groups and trade-union organs, the local authorities from the mountain area, the mayors of the valley towns, environmental organizations and the Environment Minister (report on Italy, p 19). Similar platforms are reported, which are concerned with the river Po, the Venice lagoon and the city of Milan. It seems to be thecase in the various countries that decisions on locations are especially conducive to the formation of local conflict-regulating structures (cf the reports on the UK, p 15, and the FRG).

A special form of local networking involving "works-conversion initiatives" is reported from the Federal Republic of Germany (report on the FRG, p 8). Faced with the threat of job losses, works committees of employees and trade unions were set up, which, acting locally in close cooperation with environmentalist groups, consumer groups and the representatives of political parties, have developed product proposals geared to regional requirements and regional damage, with a view to safeguarding jobs. These cooperative efforts are informal, sporadic and case-specific. They are directed against prevailing company policy (alternative cooperative plans), and, to date, it has been possible only in a few cases to persuade managements to take part in such product-development schemes (eg the PUR project in the Federal Republic of Germany).

V. Outlook: the evolutionary dynamics of new regulatory patterns

In conclusion, I shall attempt an initial overview of the subject of widening concerns, based on the material which is to hand. As actual developments in this field are still at the multi-faceted, preliminary stage, and the material has not yet been systematized, the assessment is provisional in the extreme. It does, however, allow a first evaluation to be made of the evolutionary dynamics of corporate environmental policy, and its linkage with industrial relations.

In the first place, the reports furnish few examples of the beginnings of a cooperative policy between the social partners in matters of environmental protection. A major cause - apart from the refusal of liability and traditional paradigms for the attribution of blame - lies in the fact that the **social partners have different standpoints** on the subject of the environment. The mechanism by which the issue is reformulated has already been mentioned. The employers' and employees' organizations seize on those aspects of the environmental issue which are directly linked to their central interests. The management side is concerned to safeguard competitiveness and sufficient profits, largely by projecting a favourable image among clients. The trade unions are concerned with jobs, and with health and safety. The relationship is somewhat out of balance, in that the trade unions and workers' representatives also have to support the competitiveness of the company in their own interests; if not systematically, at least in their day-to-day policy at the workplace. However, this does not look after their own particular worries, since neither the preservation of jobs nor concern for health and safety necessarily increases with rising profits. Looked at from the other side, company managements admittedly accept a degree of responsibility for staff welfare, but predominantly react only under external pressure. Only in certain countries, sectors and businesses do health and safety, beyond the essential minimum, constitute an active element of company policy. It is therefore a highly interesting question whether company managements and employers' associations will allow their concerns in this area to widen, with greater participation by trade unions and employees. For the time being, at least, the area of consensus between the actors in industrial relations on the subject of environmental initiatives is relatively narrow (cf Fig 7).

The reports make it clear that, so far, no linkage has in principle been established between protection of the environment and traditional issues. Environmental protection is added, as a marginal item, to the activities of associations and companies, as they have existed hitherto. And, crucially, this issue has not touched upon the structures or strategies in other areas. This means that prevailing strategies, which, after all, have played a part in causing environmental problems, are not being reviewed and modified in line with environmental considerations. Instead, a state of parallelism has been created, in which the generation of damage and risks is allowed to proceed side by side with marginal remedial efforts. As matters stand at present, none of the actors has met the need to assign to protection of the environment a **fully integrated and central role.**

Secondly, and this is closely linked to the above, it is apparent that there has been a considerable increase in the range of actors concerned. In every country, there are a growing number of examples in which communes, environmental groups/organizations and outside intermediaries are being drawn into company-related conflicts on the environment. In the relationships between the actors, a number of patterns seem to be emerging, which recur in the various EC countries. These are exemplified by a **universal distinction between environmental protection internal and external to the plant,** which is mainly asserted on the trade-union side. The fact that statutory provisions on rights to information and participation are restricted to a company's internal working conditions suggests that, as a first step, the demand that these rights be extended to environmental issues should be limited to the space occupied by the company. A further consideration is that external company activities (products and marketing) have until now been a decision-making area reserved solely to company management, and so constitute a rigid industrial-relations barrier. For most trade unions, it is also true that they are not actively concerned with questions of the quality of life outside the company, these issues having been entrusted to consumer associations and the green movement (as, for example, in the Federal Republic of Germany). It follows that there is no tradition of **cooperation above company level, eg with local authorities and associations** or with environmental groups, and that such cooperation has tended to be rejected, from the point of view of the trade unions' social image.

Companies themselves admittedly have strong bilateral links with the authorities, but they also stress their autonomy vis-à-vis third parties.

However, it is a characteristic of major environmental problems that their formulation (also) takes place externally to companies, and so automatically involves outside actors. Here, a number of **typical formations of factions** are discernible.

There is, for instance, as mentioned earlier, the formation by the social partners of factions within the company in the face of the outside world, ie of questions and criticisms from outside. An effort is made to keep silent for as long as possible, to allow public attention to run out of steam, or not to arise in the first place. This strategy often involves active coalitions between company managements and workers' representatives.

A second cluster of alliances forms around company management. Company managements routinely cooperate with licensing and supervisory authorities. On ecological questions and their solution, they increasingly seek to collaborate with their suppliers, whose products make up a substantial portion of the company's ecological input. Finally, company managements enlist their customers' support for their solutions.

On the other side, we find clusters of alliances forming around the trade unions. Often, the unions can count on only very weak support from the workplace (employees and workers' representatives). In contrast to their policy in the 1970s, the unions are specifically seeking contacts with environmentalists and, of course, the local authorities. Partly because of increasing local restrictions, a slight trend towards regionalization is perceptible in trade-union policy.

As far as the alignments of the actors are concerned, three points are important: the involvement of actors external to the companies; the common reference to central government by both companies and trade unions; and the narrow area of common ground (the alliance between management and works council referred to first generally operates against the natural environment) (cf Fig 8).

Thirdly, the reports give few indications that any new, cooperative forms of regulation are developing in the area of company-related environmental protection. The environmental policies of some companies are becoming broader and more aggressive, and this is true of an increasing number of company associations, with a marked concentration in the chemical and metalworking industries. The programmes are not directed at workers' representatives or the trade unions, which are, as a rule, explicitly bypassed. Cooperation occurs only here and there on a voluntary basis, and any extension of trade-union rights in matters of company environmental policy is largely rejected. Whereas the unions' target is extended statutory rights, companies focus their attention on voluntary agreements (eg sectoral agreements relating to particular pollutants or environmental technologies) and the ecological aspects of corporate planning based on clean technologies. Once again, the area of consensus is therefore relatively narrow, the emphasis being placed on verified compliance with legislation and conditions, the improvement of environmental audits, and the increased use of environmental officers in the plant (cf Fig 9).

There are two reasons why it is virtually impossible, as yet, to present the results of this research. First, the available reports provide only a preliminary insight into a new area of analysis and policy, and this will have to be deepened and systematized in further stages, which have already been initiated. Second, it lies in the nature of the evolutionary dynamics of the process by which industrial relations are rendered more responsive to the environment that more far-reaching statements cannot really be made at this moment.

A central result of this initial research phase is that, in all the countries under consideration, we are at the point of transition from the latent to the regulatory phase. The beginning of the regulatory phase is characterized by a multiplicity of interests and plans for the amendment of existing regulations and the setting-up of new regulatory systems, which are not yet coordinated, tried out, or in many cases even approved.

It is apparent that:

- the social partners, collectively and individually, accept the need for the active incorporation of environmental considerations into their own policies, and have taken the first steps to this end, ie by means of programmes, the allocation of responsibilities and isolated, preliminary initiatives;

- enterprises are very much inclined to assign to themselves the responsibility for company environmental policy, and are ready only in exceptional cases to involve shopfloor and trade-union representatives, and then only informally;

- the environmental policy of associations and companies is generally marginal and supplementary, ie it is not geared to other policy areas where there are many practices and strategies which have actually created environmental hazards and damage;

- with regard to national legislation, it remains to be seen whether and to what extent trade-union and works representatives will in future be included in the agencies, organizations and regulatory systems responsible for environmental policy at company/plant level;

- the EC dimension, as a new basic factor determining the environmental policy of companies and society, has on the whole not yet moved into the social partners' field of vision.

Given this situation, it is understandable that the trade unions, in particular, are arguing for the activation and opening-up of industrial relations, with regard to protection of the environment, and are, indeed, taking some action in this direction. Central demands are, firstly, that rights to information and participation should be given to employees and workers' representatives, and, secondly, that information and reporting systems should be established, which provide everybody with a clear insight into the way in which company activities impinge on ecosystems (environmental auditing). The last-named demand for environmental auditing is clearly receiving growing support from ecologically minded company managements.

Although the trade unions consistently demand that the remit of the agencies responsible for health and safety at work should be extended, there is no sign that this demand is supported by company managements or employers' associations. It is therefore by no means certain that the essential advances in this direction can be made in the immediate future.

The reports do not yet pay adequate attention to the question of how the development of company environmental policy ties up with developments in other areas of corporate policy. Both the debate on new corporate cultures and the discussions about new forms of employee participation, in the introduction and development of new technologies, for example, are generating considerable impetus, which is likely to influence the acceptance by companies of the environmental issue, and the participation of employees in devising strategies and practices with environmental implications. It is possible that these two elements of policy, which an increasing number of companies have developed, from a proper apprehension of their own best interests and in counteraction to authoritarian styles of management and Taylorist forms of organization, and which offer the trade unions the opportunity of introducing concepts of their own, also provide solid bases for increasing the ecological awareness of company policy.

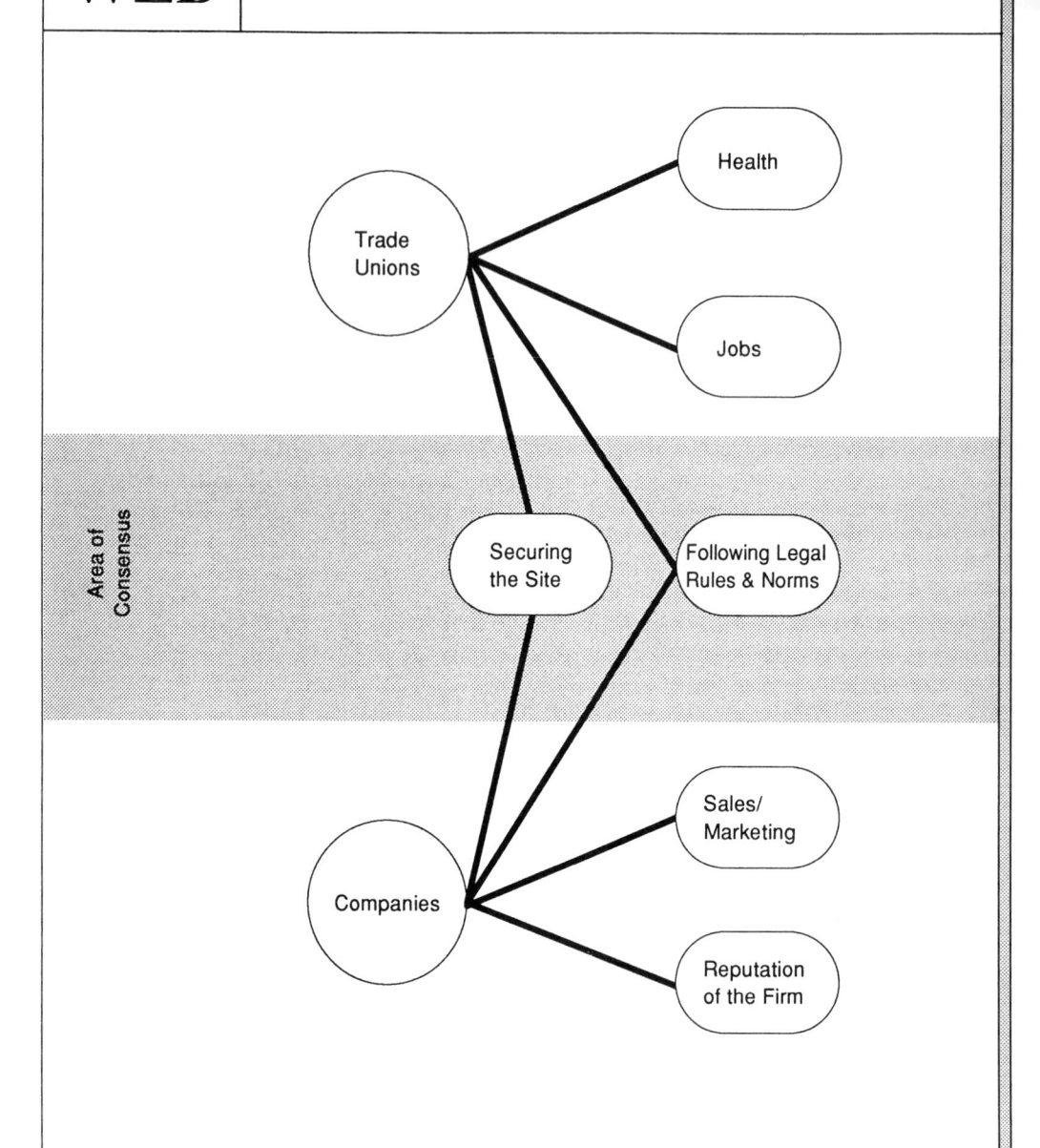

Different Strategic References to Eco-political Initiatives in the System of IR

Fig. 7

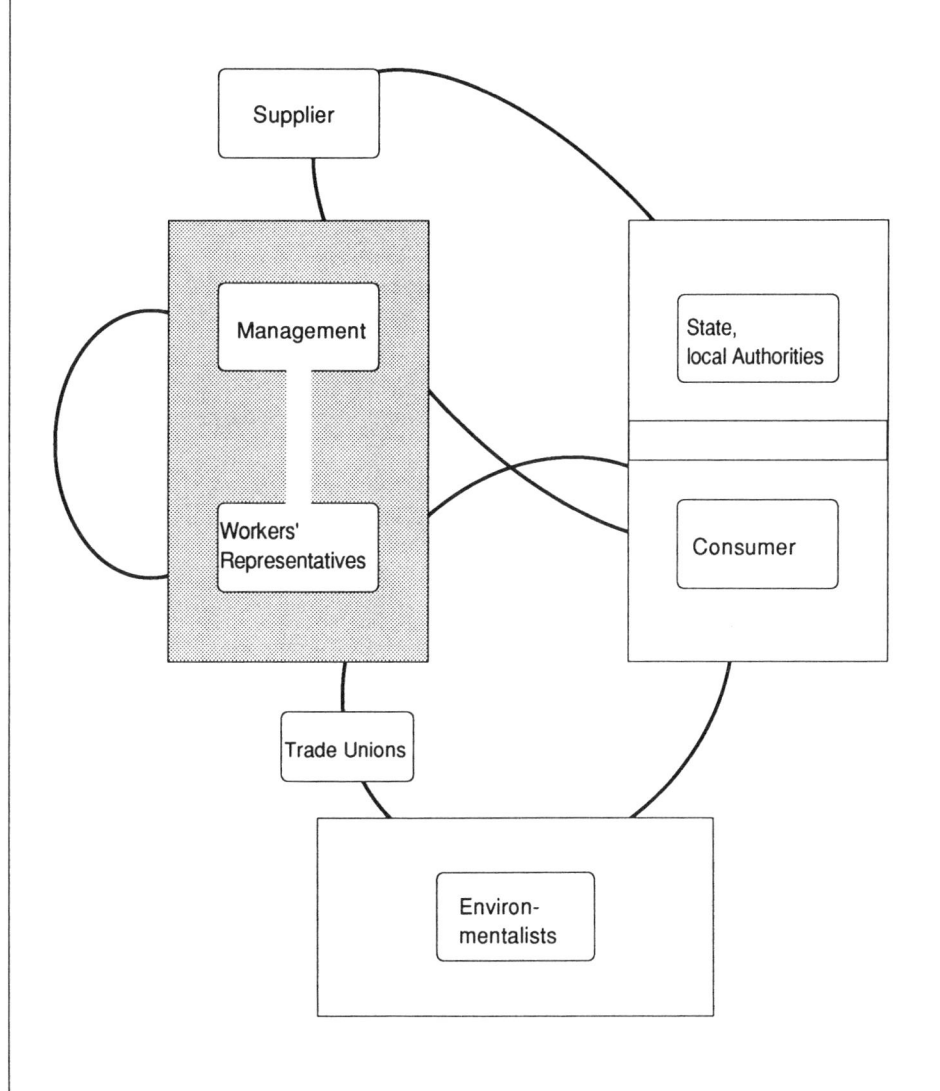

Alliances in the Environmental Actors System — **Fig. 8**

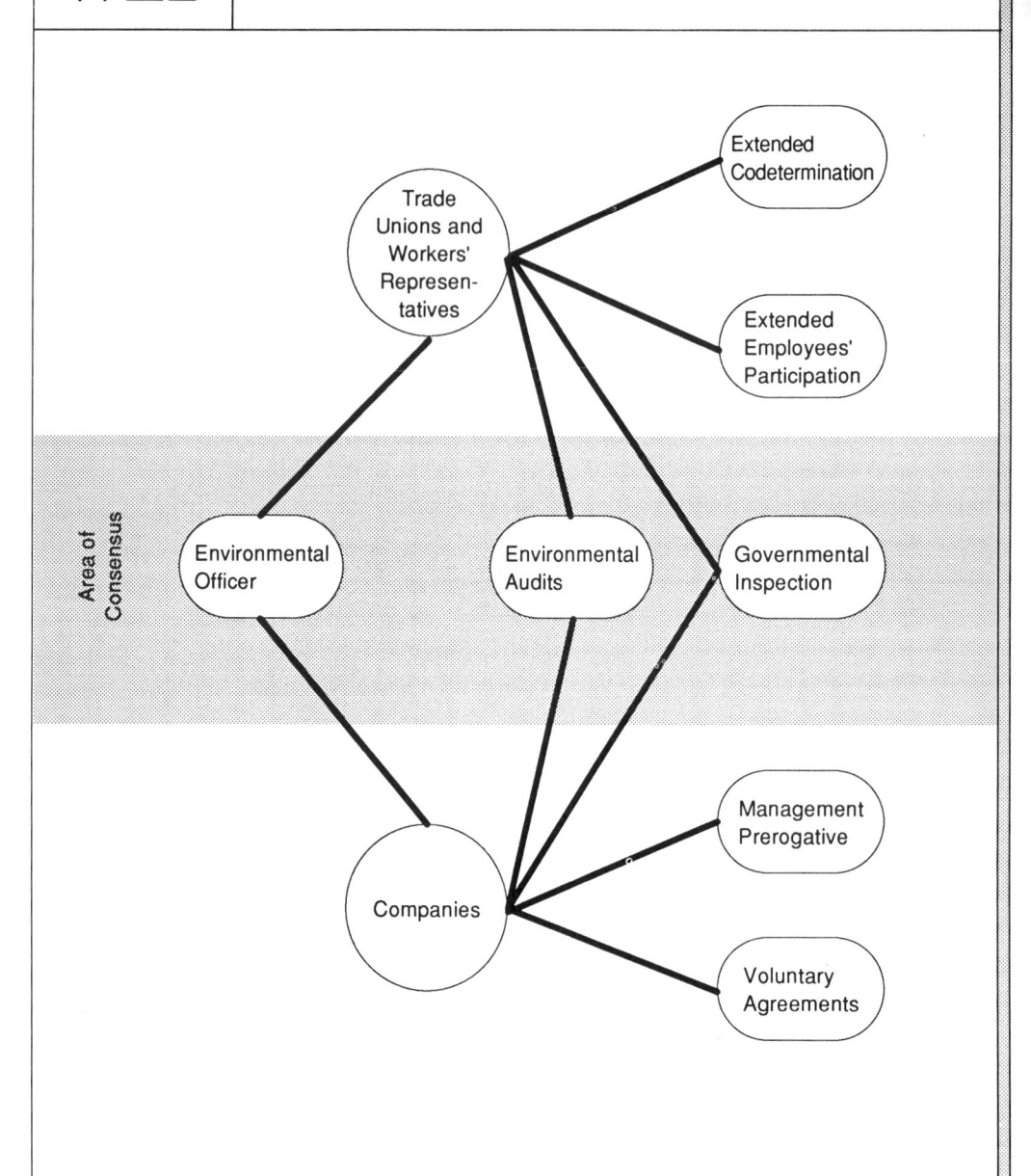

Different Modes of Regulating the environment by the System of IR

Fig. 9

Bibliography

Guido Baglioni, Colin Crouch (ed): European industrial relations - the challenge of flexibility, London, Nebury Park, New Dehli, 1990

Jan Bongaerts: Die Entwicklung der europäischen Umweltpolitik (The development of European environmental policy), in: WSI-Mitteilungen 10/1989, pp 575-584, 1989

EG-Binnenmarkt und Umweltschutz 1990 (EC internal market and environmental protection 1990), in: ifo-Schnelldienst 16-17/90

European Foundation (publ): Working for a better environment, Dublin, 1989

Förderkreis Umwelt future eV: Europa '93 - Mehr Umsatz, weniger Umweltschutz? (Europe '93 - higher turnover, less environmental protection?), Lengerich, 1990

Christian Hey, Jutta Jahns-Böhm: Ökologie und freier Binnenmarkt (Ecology and free internal market), Freiburg, 1989

Wolfgang Hoffmann-Riem: Interessenausgleich durch Verhandlungslösungen (The reconciliation of interests by negotiated solutions), in: ZAU 1/1990, pp 19-35

Harald Hohmann: Die Entwicklung der internationalen Umweltpolitik und des Umweltrechts durch internationale und europäische Organisationen (The development of international environmental policy and environmental legislation by international and European organizations), in: Aus Politik und Zeitgeschichte, vol 47-48/89, pp 29-45

Rolf Jaeger: Arbeitnehmervertretung und Arbeitnehmerrechte in den Unternehmen Westeuropas (Employees' representation and rights in the companies of Western Europe), in: Der Betriebsrat 5/1990, p 133 f; 1/1991, p 188 ff

Martin Jänicke: Erfolgsbedingungen von Umweltpolitik im internationalen Vergleich (Conditions determining the success of environmental policy - an international comparison), in: ZU 3/90, pp 213-232

Reinhold Konstanty, Bruno Zwingemann: Aussicht auf höhere Standards in der Arbeitswelt? (Prospects of higher standards in the working world?), in: Die Mitbestimmung 4/91, pp 266-270

Walther Müller-Jentsch (ed): Zukunft der Gewerkschaften - ein internationaler Vergleich (The future of the trade unions - an international comparison), Frankfurt am Main, New York, 1988

von Prittwitz: Das Katastrophen-Paradox - Elemente einer Theorie der Umweltpolitik (The catastrophe paradox - elements of a theory of environmental policy), Opladen, 1990

Schwerpunkt: Arbeitnehmer in Europa 1990 (Focal point: employees in Europe 1990), in: Die Mitbestimmung 12/90

Task force report on the environment and the internal market: "1992" The Environmental Dimension, Bonn, 1990

European Foundation for the Improvement of Living and Working Conditions

Industrial Relations and the Environment in the E.C.

Luxembourg: Office for Official Publications of the European Communities, 1992

1992 — 58 p. — 23.5 cm × 16 cm

ISBN 92-826-4687-4

Price (excluding VAT) in Luxembourg: ECU 7,50

Venta y suscripciones • Salg og abonnement • Verkauf und Abonnement • Πωλήσεις και συνδρομές
Sales and subscriptions • Vente et abonnements • Vendita e abbonamenti
Verkoop en abonnementen • Venda e assinaturas

BELGIQUE / BELGIË

**Moniteur belge /
Belgisch Staatsblad**
Rue de Louvain 42 / Leuvenseweg 42
1000 Bruxelles / 1000 Brussel
Tél. (02) 512 00 26
Fax 511 01 84
CCP / Postrekening 000-2005502-27

Autres distributeurs /
Overige verkooppunten

**Librairie européenne/
Europese Boekhandel**
Avenue Albert Jonnart 50 /
Albert Jonnartlaan 50
1200 Bruxelles / 1200 Brussel
Tél. (02) 734 02 81
Fax 735 08 60

Jean De Lannoy
Avenue du Roi 202 /Koningslaan 202
1060 Bruxelles / 1060 Brussel
Tél. (02) 538 51 69
Télex 63220 UNBOOK B
Fax (02) 538 08 41

CREDOC
Rue de la Montagne 34 / Bergstraat 34
Bte 11 / Bus 11
1000 Bruxelles / 1000 Brussel

DANMARK

**J. H. Schultz Information A/S
EF-Publikationer**
Ottiliavej 18
2500 Valby
Tlf. 36 44 22 66
Fax 36 44 01 41
Girokonto 6 00 08 86

BR DEUTSCHLAND

Bundesanzeiger Verlag
Breite Straße
Postfach 10 80 06
5000 Köln 1
Tel. (02 21) 20 29-0
Telex ANZEIGER BONN 8 882 595
Fax 20 29 278

GREECE/ΕΛΛΑΔΑ

G.C. Eleftheroudakis SA
International Bookstore
Nikis Street 4
10563 Athens
Tel. (01) 322 63 23
Telex 219410 ELEF
Fax 323 98 21

ESPAÑA

Boletín Oficial del Estado
Trafalgar, 27
28010 Madrid
Tel. (91) 44 82 135

Mundi-Prensa Libros, S.A.
Castelló, 37
28001 Madrid
Tel. (91) 431 33 99 (Libros)
     431 32 22 (Suscripciones)
     435 36 37 (Dirección)
Télex 49370-MPLI-E
Fax (91) 575 39 98

Sucursal:

Librería Internacional AEDOS
Consejo de Ciento, 391
08009 Barcelona
Tel. (93) 301 86 15
Fax (93) 317 01 41

**Llibreria de la Generalitat
de Catalunya**
Rambla dels Estudis, 118 (Palau Moja)
08002 Barcelona
Tel. (93) 302 68 35
     302 64 62
Fax (93) 302 12 99

FRANCE

**Journal officiel
Service des publications
des Communautés européennes**
26, rue Desaix
75727 Paris Cedex 15
Tél. (1) 40 58 75 00
Fax (1) 40 58 75 74

IRELAND

Government Supplies Agency
4-5 Harcourt Road
Dublin 2
Tel. (1) 61 31 11
Fax (1) 78 06 45

ITALIA

Licosa Spa
Via Duca di Calabria, 1/1
Casella postale 552
50125 Firenze
Tel. (055) 64 54 15
Fax 64 12 57
Telex 570466 LICOSA I
CCP 343 509

GRAND-DUCHÉ DE LUXEMBOURG

Messageries Paul Kraus
11, rue Christophe Plantin
2339 Luxembourg
Tél. 499 88 88
Télex 2515
Fax 499 88 84 44
CCP 49242-63

NEDERLAND

SDU Overheidsinformatie
Externe Fondsen
Postbus 20014
2500 EA 's-Gravenhage
Tel. (070) 37 89 911
Fax (070) 34 75 778

PORTUGAL

Imprensa Nacional
Casa da Moeda, EP
Rua D. Francisco Manuel de Melo, 5
1092 Lisboa Codex
Tel. (01) 69 34 14

**Distribuidora de Livros
Bertrand, Ld.ª**
Grupo Bertrand, SA
Rua das Terras dos Vales, 4-A
Apartado 37
2700 Amadora Codex
Tel. (01) 49 59 050
Telex 15798 BERDIS
Fax 49 60 255

UNITED KINGDOM

HMSO Books (PC 16)
HMSO Publications Centre
51 Nine Elms Lane
London SW8 5DR
Tel. (071) 873 2000
Fax GP3 873 8463
Telex 29 71 138

ÖSTERREICH

**Manz'sche Verlags-
und Universitätsbuchhandlung**
Kohlmarkt 16
1014 Wien
Tel. (0222) 531 61-0
Telex 11 25 00 BOX A
Fax (0222) 531 61-39

SUOMI

Akateeminen Kirjakauppa
Keskuskatu 1
PO Box 128
00101 Helsinki
Tel. (0) 121 41
Fax (0) 121 44 41

NORGE

Narvesen information center
Bertrand Narvesens vei 2
PO Box 6125 Etterstad
0602 Oslo 6
Tel. (2) 57 33 00
Telex 79668 NIC N
Fax (2) 68 19 01

SVERIGE

BTJ
Box 200
22100 Lund
Tel. (046) 18 00 00
Fax (046) 18 01 25

SCHWEIZ / SUISSE / SVIZZERA

OSEC
Stampfenbachstraße 85
8035 Zürich
Tel. (01) 365 54 49
Fax (01) 365 54 11

CESKOSLOVENSKO

NIS
Havelkova 22
13000 Praha 3
Tel. (02) 235 84 46
Fax 42-2-264775

MAGYARORSZÁG

Euro-Info-Service
Budapest I. Kir.
Attila út 93
1012 Budapest
Tel. (1) 56 82 11
Telex (22) 4717 AGINF H-61
Fax (1) 17 59 031

POLSKA

Business Foundation
ul. Krucza 38/42
00-512 Warszawa
Tel. (22) 21 99 93, 628-28-82
International Fax&Phone
(0-39) 12-00-77

JUGOSLAVIJA

Privredni Vjesnik
Bulevar Lenjina 171/XIV
11070 Beograd
Tel. (11) 123 23 40

CYPRUS

**Cyprus Chamber of Commerce and
Industry**
Chamber Building
38 Grivas Dhigenis Ave
3 Deligiorgis Street
PO Box 1455
Nicosia
Tel. (2) 449500/462312
Fax (2) 458630

TÜRKIYE

**Pres Gazete Kitap Dergi
Pazarlama Dağitim Ticaret ve sanayi
AŞ**
Narlibahçe Sokak N. 15
Istanbul-Cağaloğlu
Tel. (1) 520 92 96 - 528 55 66
Fax 520 64 57
Telex 23822 DSVO-TR

CANADA

Renouf Publishing Co. Ltd
Mail orders — Head Office:
1294 Algoma Road
Ottawa, Ontario K1B 3W8
Tel. (613) 741 43 33
Fax (613) 741 54 39
Telex 0534783

Ottawa Store:
61 Sparks Street
Tel. (613) 238 89 85

Toronto Store:
211 Yonge Street
Tel. (416) 363 31 71

UNITED STATES OF AMERICA

UNIPUB
4611-F Assembly Drive
Lanham, MD 20706-4391
Tel. Toll Free (800) 274 4888
Fax (301) 459 0056

AUSTRALIA

Hunter Publications
58A Gipps Street
Collingwood
Victoria 3066

JAPAN

Kinokuniya Company Ltd
17-7 Shinjuku 3-Chome
Shinjuku-ku
Tokyo 160-91
Tel. (03) 3439-0121

Journal Department
PO Box 55 Chitose
Tokyo 156
Tel. (03) 3439-0124

AUTRES PAYS
OTHER COUNTRIES
ANDERE LÄNDER

**Office des publications officielles
des Communautés européennes**
2, rue Mercier
2985 Luxembourg
Tél. 49 92 81
Télex PUBOF LU 1324 b
Fax 48 85 73/48 68 17
CC bancaire BIL 8-109/6003/700

12/91